Moral and Religious Education in County Primary Schools

Moral and Religious Education in County Primary Schools

Report of a Working Party to the Social Morality Council

H. J. Blackham, *editor*

NFER Publishing Company Ltd.

Published by the NFER Publishing Company Ltd.,
2 Jennings Buildings, Thames Avenue,
Windsor, Berks. SL4 1QS
Registered Office: The Mere, Upton Park, Slough, Berks. SL1 2DQ
First published 1976
© Social Morality Council, 1976

ISBN 0 85633 1155

Printed in Great Britain by
Biddles of Guildford, Martyr Road, Guildford, Surrey

Distributed in the USA by Humanities Press Inc.,
Atlantic Highlands, New Jersey 07716 USA.

Contents

Working Party on Moral and Religious Education in County Primary Schools

(The descriptions refer to positions held at the time of the working party.)

S.N. Bharadwaj (Hindu)	President, Hindu Centre, Kilburn
H.J. Blackham (Humanist) (*Chairman*)	Chairman, Executive Committee, Social Morality Council
L.G. Buxton (Humanist)	Staff Inspector, Inner London Education Authority
Miss Eileen Drakley(Methodist)	Headmistress, Virginia Primary (J M & I) School, London E2 [Died before the conclusion of the working party.]
Miss Janet Eavis (Quaker)	Headmistress, Tufnell Park Primary School, London N7
E.G. Faregrave (C of E)	Headmaster, Pakeman Junior School, N7
Mrs Betty Harris (Humanist)	Headmistress, Star County Infant School, E16
A. Head (Agnostic)	Headmaster, William Tyndale Junior School, N1
Rev David Konstant (RC)	Director, Westminster Religious Education Centre
Rev Philip Lee-Woolf (Congregationalist)	General Secretary, Christian Education Movement
E. Oliver (RC)	Secretary General, Social Morality Council
G.V. Pape (Methodist) (Observer)	Staff Inspector for Junior Education, Inner London Education Authority

F. Rose (Jewish)   Headmaster,
                                    Millfield Junior School, E5

M.J. Sherwani (Muslim)   Assistant Master,
                                    Crampton Junior School

Miss R. Standeven (C of E)   Lecturer, Balls Park College
                                    of Education, Hertford

M.W. Stephenson (C of E)   Headmaster,
                                    Bredinghurst School, SE15

Sister Joyce Webb (RC)   Lecturer,
                                    Mary Ward College of Education

Rev Peter Wetz (RC)   Lecturer,
                                    Corpus Christi College, W11

Mrs Pamela Wylam (Sikh)

This report is the work of a group composed mainly of teachers in infant and junior schools, all of whom were in agreement with the report published by the Social Morality Council in 1970, *Moral and Religious Education in County Schools*. That report made history, in the sense that it registered the first policy agreement of its kind between educators representative of religious belief and of non-religious humanism. It was quoted, along with the Durham Report, in a Parliamentary debate in March 1971[1] and was commended by the Government of the day as pointing the way forward. The Government spokesman confirmed at the time that a further report was expected from the same source.

The one criticism generally made of the report was that its signatories numbered too few people currently engaged in teaching. The same cannot be said of this second report. It is concerned with both policy and practice and offers some help in the classroom, although it is not a resource book. Even during the two years in which the group was meeting regularly, the open approach to moral and religious education recommended here became more widely accepted. (And since then publication has been unduly delayed for reasons outside our control.) The special value of the report is in the diversity of basic convictions represented by the signatories.

The policy underlying moral and religious education in these pages is one of the general aims of education currently accepted, 'growth towards autonomy'.[2] Such an aim is contrary to the policy and discipline of education in some other countries, eg, the Soviet Union;[3] and even to the practice and expectations of education in this country not many years ago.[4] Developments in our society and within educational theory and research have given emphasis to personal autonomy as an educational aim. We firmly believe that respect for a child's independence and help in growth towards autonomy can hardly begin too soon and can never be less important than acquisition of knowledge and skills socially required. Indeed, the two help one another.

Each section was drafted by a different hand, and all were fully discussed by the group in the course of our regular meetings. They were amended in discussion, and rewritten in consequence of discussion. The material was at the end submitted for comment to several colleagues. We are grateful to them for their criticism, and particularly to Mr John Burrows, CBE, HM Chief Inspector for Primary Education, 1966–73. Subsequently, the material was revised and edited for presentation in this report, with the consent of the group. Distinctions of style in the original drafts remain. The essentials of Part One are easily grasped. Part Two provides suggestions for teachers in applying them to the curriculum.

H J B

Notes
1. GREAT BRITAIN PARLIAMENT. (1971) *Hansard,* 316, 80, 1409—43.
2. DEARDEN, R.F. (1968). *The Philosophy of Primary Education.* London: Routledge and Kegan Paul.
3. BRONFENBRENNER, U. (1971). *Two Worlds of Childhood: USA and USSR.* London: Allen & Unwin.
4. CALVERT, B. (1975). *The Role of the Pupil.* London: Routledge & Kegan Paul.

Part One

Chapter One

Principles and Aims

Stages of moral development
The earliest years before the child comes even to nursery school are highly important for moral development, and are not to be considered 'pre-moral' when nothing positive has to be done to educate the child. His treatment from the beginning makes a lasting impression on him, and helps to form his response to the world. In learning to do things for himself and to be himself, as in learning to stand and to walk on his own, a child at this early period fluctuates between failure and success, self-assertion and a return to dependence. He needs both support and freedom, to submit to control and conform to requirements and to rebel against them and internalize the control as his own. About the age of two there may be a specially defiant struggle for independence which seems to anticipate adolescence, and which demands specially tolerant latitude and understanding support.

If a child has not had the security of constant affection at home, if he has been or has felt rejected, or if he has been treated inconsistently, the basic conditions for normal moral development will be lacking. Something can be done in nursery and infant schools to provide the conditions of a stable background, with consistent external requirements and controls and freedom to try things out and follow his own line. The school is a structured situation which gives needed support and encouragement as well as restraint, and at the same time the child has the freedom to discover and explore the world around and come to terms with himself and with others.

In the junior school his peers should normally mean more to him than the adults in the background. Through group activities he learns to be reliable in social interdependence, and at the same time is helped to gain his footing of independence of the adult generation. He is seeking an identity and a social role and relationships in competitive and cooperative enterprises with his peers. He is counted on and counts on others, helps and is helped.

The work of moral education is to safeguard and develop both the vitality and personal independence of the child and his ability and readiness to be reliably and amiably cooperative. Conflicts between his claims and those of others or group requirements, which mean also conflicts within himself, are inevitable and may be severe and destructive. Such conflicts and tensions are relieved in the earliest years by external adult control, which should always be firm and never be frightening. This is the necessary condition of the child's learning to control himself. Similarly, in group situations adults intervene in 'squabbles'. In these ways the child learns to own and own up to his own acts, to acknowledge the equal claims of others, and to appreciate the requirements and the advantages of a moral order.

These elements of morality are learned and reinforced at home and at school under the influence of many adults and peers, and in contexts of increasing range with the development of the child's physical and mental powers and multiplying interests. The developmental moral behaviour of the child will vary with the methods of education applied to him (e.g, authoritative or open), for he will adapt his behaviour as best he can to meet his own needs and wants; but he is not likely to become morally responsible in the sense of responsive to the claims of others and the requirements of a moral order unless he finds a secure and equal place with others in that order. Morality can be taught to any purpose only insofar as it is sustained by genuine mutuality.

Foundations

In the preparatory work of primary education foundations are laid (in understanding, in dispositions and attitudes, in skills) on which building can go on during the secondary phase and later throughout life. Therefore, the teacher should be wary of teaching at this time what may later be rejected. In concession to the immaturity of the child for fear of confusing him, to shield him from the controversies and uncertainties of later life for which he is not ready, it may seem right or necessary to ignore difficulties or to pretend that things are other than they are. Indeed, the child himself is only too ready to have it that way. His morality is likely to be absolute in black and white terms: this is always and everywhere right, and to be practised and praised; that is always and everywhere wrong, and to be avoided and condemned. People are bad or good. For very young children the good and the bad are known simply as what makes grown-ups pleased or cross. The teacher, who knows very well that this is the child's unknowing travesty of morality, should be wary of reinforcing these tendencies. For example, it is far more important that the child should learn to consider the interests and feelings of others (and try to get others to consider his own) than that he should be encouraged to praise and to blame and to label behaviour 'good' or 'bad'. Moral attitudes and judgments are unavoidable, but for that very reason they should be discouraged rather than reinforced when they are inevitably immature. By the same token, the adult needs to be doubly careful in applying them to a young child.

Correspondingly in RE, it may seem necessary to assume or to teach the Christian faith as the belief of the school and of the adult world. (The majority of the Plowden Committee took this line: 'They should be taught to know and love God . . . They should not be confused by being taught to doubt before faith is established.'[1]) It has seemed to some a betrayal of the very young to teach them less than this, leaving them to learn in their own good time to modify the teaching if they must.

Any approach which in good faith and out of consideration for the immaturity of the child misrepresents the truth of the situation, whether in morality or in religion, is pedagogically mistaken and morally wrong. It is also unnecessary. Children in the primary school can learn to understand, to feel and respond, and to behave, in ways that will serve them for the rest of their lives, whatever particular convictions they will eventually form. The foundations of moral and religious education can and should be general and at the same time concrete, taking account of the particular patterns of thought or practice of the families from which the children come.

Foundations in primary moral and religious education can be laid in three main types of learning: learning *that* (learning to understand, cognition); learning *to* (acquiring a settled disposition in response to certain general situations); learning *how* (acquiring a skill).

To look first at moral education in these terms. The young child of course has rudimentary moral notions, a growing sense of fairness and unfairness, an understanding through experience of the meaning of a helping hand or a cold shoulder. The foundation here is to understand the basic moral situation in terms of social interdependence and personal independence, with the tension between them and the indefeasible claims of both. This understanding can be the result of a little reflection and discussion arising out of innumerable experiences occasioned by material in the curriculum or episodes in the school or events outside — examples of a conflict of interests. In this context of understanding, a fellow-feeling for others as persons like oneself, a readiness to consider their feelings and interests equally with one's own, is a disposition which can be encouraged and reinforced. In the same context of understanding, the skills of reaching agreement and of loyal cooperation can be learned; balanced by learned self-reliance and encouraged initiatives. Laying such foundations deeply and firmly, adults have no need to hide their own uncertainties nor to pretend that anything is other than it is. Education is always education in the truth, whatever it may be, even when the truth is uncertainty.

Religious education should follow the same course in the primary situation. Children should learn of the different religious practices and beliefs in the world long before they can understand the meaning behind them. This diversity will worry them only if the grown-ups are worried. Otherwise, young children are natural anthropologists, interested in different ways of living as they can perceive them. They do not have to make commitments, and use should be made of this detachment to make them acquainted without anxiety with the diversity there is in ways of thinking and living. This is not education in toleration, but it is preparation for a mature acceptance of human differences.

In the realm of response and disposition (learning *to*), the specifically religious responses (awe, gratitude, worship) can be cultivated in the most general and spontaneous way through expressive arts and through loving relations in the group, as well as through a variety of community celebrations. The important thing at this stage is to stimulate and aid expression of actual feeling and response.

In the realm of skills (learning *how*), the specifically religious ones for the adult are prayer, meditation, and the like. Here the general feature is detachment from the daily rush of affairs, the busyness of life, from domination by the rational and the practical, so that one is in touch with resources within and without which otherwise remain inaccessible. Play and fantasy, which have so large a part in the life of children and help them to assimilate and make use of their experience in coming to terms with the world, may in their openness and liberation be nearer in function to prayer and meditation than is usually recognized. The new freedom of artistic expression, as opposed to the old regimentation in drawing, is of course an acknowledgement and cultivation of this general function.

The all-important point to be made about laying foundations of moral and religious education is that they ought to be permanent foundations, not the remains of eroded traditions. At this stage, it is possible and profitable to be both general and concrete, and this is the only way in which to build to last in a world continuously exposed to challenge, change, and uncertainty.

Aims

What should have been done for the child in moral and religious education by the time he leaves the junior school? The assessment is not so much in terms of knowledge acquired as of experience leading to the kind of understanding, dispositions, and skills which have been indicated: an understanding and acceptance of the requirements of social interdependence; a sense of identity and worth as the basis of personal independence; a fellow-feeling for the other as a person with equal claims; proved reliability in social roles; a personal response to the world which has been stimulated and developed by the cultivation of sensitivity and awareness.

The experience which can yield such moral results is basically an induction into creative groups at each level of education which encourage and aid initiative and at the same time have requirements (roles, rules, tasks) which are not rigid nor imposed but are inexorable in the sense that such requirements are the conditions of human existence. The experience of these conditions is not conceptualized at this stage; but insufficient care in laying the social and emotional foundations can hardly be remedied later.

Similarly, his religious education should have made the child more open to the world, more imaginative, more sensitive, more responsive, more questioning, not furnished with ready-made grown-up answers. This is the time for throwing open windows on the world. Everyone is all too liable to shut himself up in his own convictions. Education at least delays this event by enlarging the view. Whatever tends to foreclose the question, the religious question, stultifies religious education.

The practical test of primary education is whether or not the child goes on to the secondary school eager and able to play his part in the life of the school. A child who has run willingly to his primary schools because encouraged, stimulated, and developed by his treatment there has had the best start in life teachers can give him.

Notes

1. DEPARTMENT OF EDUCATION AND SCIENCE: CENTRAL ADVISORY COUNCIL FOR EDUCATION (ENGLAND) (1967). *Children and their Primary Schools*. (Plowden Report), 1, para. 572. London: HMSO.

Chapter Two

The School Community

Who compose the school community?
Answers to this question depend on whom within the community we ask. Members of each of the constituent groups have a different perspective, and perhaps each view has its own validity. We might first follow the child on his way to school, and see the people he meets. The first encounter is likely to be with a school friend, who goes along with him. If there is a busy road to cross as they near school, they may meet the 'lollipop' man. To the child he may appear as a bogey figure or as a cheerful friend, either another unpredictable and often irritable adult seeking to restrict his freedom or someone who offers warmth and security. The local policeman may be there if the school has encouraged him to visit them, to establish that policemen can be turned to in trouble.

The playground can be a turbulent place, upsetting for the young and timid, offering opportunities for showing off to the bolder spirits. The presence of a single persecuting enemy can turn it into a jungle, and the frightened child may seek to circle near the teacher on duty. To others, the same teacher may be the subject of whispered stories that gather around authority figures.

The schoolkeeper may be about. He often presents a strong and imposing figure with an authority beyond and above that of a mere teacher.

In school, his own teacher takes him over, for him the most significant person in the school community, who will condition his whole attitude towards school. He may move through a team-teaching situation, be a member of a segregated group, or be involved in other groups of various size, but at the primary school level there is a clear need for a sound and stable relationship with one adult.

At the school assembly, even in the least authoritarian school, the head makes his or her own impact on the child, an influence that should grow as the child moves up the school and provide a continuity throughout his time there.

In the classroom there may be other adults, indeed there should be; the infant or junior helper, a parent lending a hand, a student observing or helping. There are still schools where the classrooms have firmly closed doors, but in most the child will be in contact with a variety of people. Contact, unqualified, is not enough. If in all of them he can feel affection, there is an important addition to the rewarding experience school can be. If not, if the child is merely confronted with adults who one after another try to impose their unclear wishes upon him, he will be confused and feel insecure.

Yet more adults appear at lunch time: the dinner ladies, serving or supervising his meal, and the helpers in the playground, providing a quick service for hurt knees and wounded feelings.

At some time during the day, particularly if the child has occasion to visit the head, he will see the school secretary sitting at her typewriter or counting piles of money or bustling around the school. Perhaps he wonders how important she is, and his first question about authority relationships within the school begins to be formulated. One young teacher we know asked each of her class to put in order of 'importance' the people whom they met during the day. On most of the lists the headmaster came first, although on some he was displaced by the schoolkeeper, who invariably, in racing terms, 'ran well'. The teacher who played the piano at assembly was worth an each-way bet for a place in the first three. Her unique position on the occasion when the community were gathered together clearly made its mark. The school secretary was seen as a person of significance, perhaps because she collected so much money. At this particular school, the cook was not formidable enough or remained too secluded in her fortress to appear on any list. This young teacher was relieved to find that she did rank well on some lists, although on too many she appeared in a station of life that reflected a view of herself she had begun to suspect.

We have spent some time on this 'child's eye' view of the school because it does have a special relevance. The child is our central concern, and his view of the situation in which we put him is of great importance to his education. We have seen how many contacts he has to encompass, whether or not he needs to understand the role of each of these adults. Any community of adults is a complex network of personal and authority relationships, of which the child need know little. It is only when he is presented with conflicting demands by different adults that these relationships do obtrude on his attention. If he is made uncertain whom he should obey, he is brought under stress. When all adults regard their primary function as helping the child, his need to understand their relationships recedes.

The child makes contact with all parts of the school community because that community is devised for him. Those who are not pupils have perhaps less regular contact with all other groups, and inevitably on occasions tend to disregard them. There is often a lack of cohesion among teaching staff, the schoolkeeper and his helpers, the meals staff, and the 'office' (perhaps a part-time secretary).

Particularly, there is the danger that the teacher may have a lop-sided view of the community. Rightly proud of his/her own professionalism, he/she may be less aware of the skills that others need to perform their functions. Directly concerned as teachers are with the central purpose of the school, the education of the child, they may interpret this too narrowly and fail to see the influence others have on the child's development. Those of us who are teachers may have a lingering feeling that because what we do is so important to education, what others do must be subsidiary or peripheral. Some teachers might answer the question that heads this section: 'The children and their teachers'. Regrettably, the school assembly tends to reinforce this view. It is intended as an expression of the community, and yet it usually excludes so many of them. The kitchen staff may contribute a clatter of plates, but real involvement is rare.

A head has perhaps the best single view of the whole community. Like the child, he/she comes across all its parts during the day, and needs to understand those forces which unite it and the tensions which threaten it. His special position should help him to sense the atmosphere and to make the subtle interventions which ensure that care and concern manifestly prevail. He must lead his team and on occasions take final decisions, but his moves must eventually meet the wishes of the community.

On promotion to a headship a teacher needs to make many adjustments, and one of the most difficult is the widening of outlook needed to encompass far more than the teaching aspect of the school with which he was previously preoccupied. No experienced head could possibly undervalue the role of, say, the schoolkeeper or the school secretary. This is not to say that the head's view is always the most relevant. The danger of heads who suffer from a god-complex is too well known to need comment, but the position itself is the vantage-point for a comprehensive and balanced view. The schoolkeeper, too, has relations with all parts of the community, so that his standpoint makes his views of special interest.

Can we combine these pictures of the school community in a simple diagram? We could place the child at the centre of concentric circles which show nearest to him those most closely connected with his school day, and in the outer circles the more occasional visitors, such as inspectors and educational psychologists. An alternative might be a hierarchical family tree with the head at the apex, though the tangle of weak and strong authority relations and the connexions outside the school would produce a web that did not make all things clear.

In particular, what is the role of parents? An effective school must involve its parents and express their desires for the education of their children, but should they be thought of as members of the community or as special guests? Though their main base is not in the school, their influence cannot be overestimated, and we hope to see them as an increasing presence in our schools. Perhaps we should have started from the local community and looked at the place of the school within it, but if we are to discuss in the main the activities of the school, this more general approach lacks the appropriate focus.

In the end we gave it up. Many folk in and around the school have been mentioned. They, and doubtless others, belong to the school community more or less intimately, and this list with the discussion involved perhaps identifies the community better than any categorization or schema could.

Attitudes within the community

Once a community is established which has within it separate groups, we have only to wait for 'us' and 'them' attitudes to appear. Left unchecked, these attitudes develop into warring camps, with shifting alliances. Who prevents this, and how?

The answer to the first part is 'everyone', though perhaps the single person who can do most, and is certainly expected to do most, is the head. Before everything, he must carefully reject the role of warleader of the teaching staff that some might be eager to thrust upon him.

The first need, we have suggested, is mutual understanding of roles. It is no use a teacher's asking the schoolkeeper in very positive terms to do something, if it is not his job or if it is no business of the teacher. If the schoolkeeper told a teacher that he ought to do dinner duty, similar feelings would be aroused. The teacher's professional role is a special one, which cannot be filled by anyone else, but others contribute also to the creation of the school environment, as we have seen in trying to put together those who belong to the school community. People do not always want to know what others do, even when what they do is closely linked with their own activities. However, it is possible to make tensions productive. The resolution of a row between two people can result in their both learning; in particular, each learns what feature of the other's function has been trespassed upon or underrated. It is not, of course, always the head who resolves tensions, although his position is such that resolution is easier if attempted by him. A skilled conciliator can explain to each antagonist why the other is angry.

Links can be encouraged at other times. A head may sometimes ask a teacher to negotiate with the schoolkeeper in connexion with an evening function, so that the two may get to know each other in a situation where an amicable arrangement can be readily arrived at.

Too often groups become aware of each other only when there is a grievance and one feels let down in some way. Occasions should be sought more frequently when all involved in the community can be seen to be taking part. There is a number of times during the school year when the school is 'on show', and on these public occasions it can be shown, very easily, that everyone matters.

One secondary school known to us conducts seminars for its young teachers. During some of the sessions, different people who have connexions with the school discuss their jobs; some are from outside the immediate school community, others from inside. Such smallish group sessions, mainly question and answer, can give useful insights. Whether or not the same possibility exists in a primary school may be arguable, but could not staff meetings consist, sometimes, of such a discussion? Even this would suggest that the teaching staff is not the one real consultative body, and that it now and again seeks to inform itself of the activities of others. How many staff meetings in a school regularly include people other than teachers? The staff as a whole, teaching and non-teaching, might well be involved in a general discussion about ways of keeping the school clean and tidy. Perhaps there are several such general matters which cannot be effectively discussed by the teaching staff alone. Larger establishments in further and higher education have statutory committees which include representatives of all sections of the community, so that the body can indeed function in its unity through the communication and cooperation of its members.

Understanding the roles of others is an important beginning, but fellow feeling is often damaged by the growth of status struggles and attempts to alter the relative importance of roles. As with other tensions, there is nothing necessarily bad here, for it is through such struggles and reappraisals that societies develop, even on the small scale of a school. But when these struggles result in denigrations, nothing but ill feeling is produced. In the end, any readjustment should be related to the probable effect on the development of the children.

Discussions of the roles laid down in the running of the school, healthy and productive of growth when properly managed, can do only harm if comment on the role begins or ends with animosity towards the person, or with disparagement. Any thinking teacher knows from his classroom experience that personal inadequacy is usually best helped by encouragement, rather than by direct and forceful criticism — which seldom fails to be also scornful. Community living contributes positively to moral education only insofar as respect for persons is maintained.

Attitudes in class towards academic performance are of special significance. Too often we use the words 'good' and 'bad' to describe such performances, with entirely inappropriate moral connotations. We should certainly encourage children to do as well as they can, but the very association of 'good' with 'able' casts doubt on the personal value of the less able. Such feelings of doubt and insecurity are reinforced by any strongly competitive element in the work.

Mutual understanding and appreciation of roles should be helped by the common purpose which brings and binds together all the adults concerned with a school, manifested in their general willingness to help, which the child experiences as care as well as control, and which by its consistency provides the basic security required for moral development.

Discipline

When the oldest generation of teachers now working in schools were at college, the reports on their teaching practice included an entry under the heading 'Discipline'. Here was assessed the candidate's ability to keep order in a classroom by inborn aptitude, force of personality, or hard-won command of the approved classroom techniques. 'Discipline' meant, on the teacher's part, the establishing of his unquestioned (desirably, benevolent) authority; and, on the pupil's part, conformity to a code of rules within the classroom and the school that kept him for the most part quiet and immobile, passive rather than active, receiving rather than giving. Under such a meaning, discipline easily became synonymous in the area of behaviour with punishment ('This child must be disciplined') and in the area of study with a tight mental control ('The discipline of Euclidean geometry'). There seems to have been a confusion between the control which is a necessary feature of organized development and the means by which such control is achieved. To equate discipline simply with a system of reward and punishment or with a systematic form of learning is to narrow and weaken its meaning.

Discipline is that part of education which is particularly concerned with growth to personal responsibility and autonomy. Many factors contribute to this process: the relationships in a school (between teachers and pupils, among the teachers, among the pupils); the degree of participation that is encouraged within the school; the extent to which initiative is recognized; imagination and creativity in the use of materials; and also the rules, regulations, and organization of the school and classroom. Assessment of a teacher's discipline is an assessment of his whole approach to education. It concerns his ability to relate to the class as a group and as individuals; his skill in organizing the classroom and the programme so that they provide concrete learning situations, rich in materials, objects, and media, awaiting selection, manipulation, and ordering by the child, whose creative impulse is released and stimulated.

Such a classroom can be a creative workshop and a school for learning; it can also, regrettably, be a formless chaos. Making of it the former demands of the teacher clearly thought out objectives and an underlying organization that allows for the full stretching and the continuous follow-up of each individual in the class, who is, nevertheless, free to work at his own rate and to follow his own lines of discovery. This calls for control. No learning is possible without it. Children need a reasonably predictable order and a reliable frame of reference. The source of this is the teacher himself who guides, encourages, and stimulates the child in the various learning situations offered. The child learns self-discipline by living in a community within which controlled growth to responsibility is possible. Each community discovers for itself the proper balance between control and growth. The discipline of the school, or individual teacher or parent, considered in the way that has been described, is a necessary condition of the child's growth to self-reliance, responsibility, and autonomy, the foundation, that is, of moral education.

The school in the community

The school as a community ought not to be separated in thought or in practice from the school in a community. Teachers who are ignorant of the language and customs of the homes from which their children come, because they themselves live elsewhere and have a different social background, are teaching to little purpose. The child is a child in a home; and nobody who does not go outside the school can achieve a 'child's eye view' of the school. The teacher needs to go into the home and into the community, and parents should be brought into the school. Communication (and therefore education) is not possible unless there is a link between the language of the school and the language of the home. The neighbourhood and the home background are important criteria in the choice of reading matter and in planning the curriculum — or the lunacy of drilling tribal Africans in the Kings of England is matched. Any unsympathetic or unthinking attempt of a school or teacher to drive a wedge between the child and his background is not likely to be successful but is most likely to do damage. The child is to be taught to live in his own environment, for any other world is likely to remain unreal to him, however much he tries to please his teacher. Ideally, he should be helped both to value his home and his neighbourhood and to see them in the light of other places and other ways, to live in them and to transcend them.

To say that the child in a school is also a child in a home and that the teacher should be concerned with both may seem to ask too much of the teacher. For example, is a middle class teacher in a school in a deprived urban area to be expected to go out of his or her way to learn to understand and make sympathetic contacts with the community of the neighbourhood, as if he or she were in the position of a social worker? The simple answer is that any teacher who does not is at a disadvantage as a teacher and leaves out the main resource for effective teaching in that place. To take a narrowly professional stand is to handicap oneself as a teacher in that particular situation and to forfeit the rewards of teaching. In particular, it is to disqualify oneself for moral education.

Chapter Three

Methods of Teaching in Relation to Moral Development

According to John Wilson and his co-workers[1] the fundamentals of moral development may be analysed into six components. They are: the ability to treat others with consideration, otherwise defined as an aspect of love; the ability to understand and identify with the feelings of others; the ability to master the facts relevant to the making of moral decisions; the ability to formulate social rules in relation to society; the ability to make rules for one's personal conduct; and the skill to put these into practice. If the ultimate aim of moral education is to produce morally autonomous adults, according to these definitions, the teaching methods employed in the primary school should be such as will provide an environment where these components can be nurtured and developed by exemplification and in practice by the children. The primary child can learn both from practical experience and from discussion. He needs enough freedom of movement and personal autonomy to be able to gain that experience. At the same time, he needs a secure, structured environment within which he can learn to live with others at the appropriate level for his age and with due consideration for the interests of others besides himself. The provision of a correct balance between child-autonomy and rules and structure, for any particular group of children, is largely a matter for the teacher's individual judgment and experience combined with the methods of organization employed in the whole school. Methods of organization will inevitably differ widely, and the question is in what way these can influence the moral development of the child.

It is necessary to be clear as to the nature of the moral development we are aiming to foster. Often, in the past, social morality has been seen as the training of the individual to conform to a number of set rules in society; to make him docile, obedient and conforming in accordance with his social position and his standard of academic education. This is no longer appropriate in a society of free and equal individuals where social interaction needs to be based upon principles of behaviour rather than upon rigid rules. The discovery of such principles is largely a matter of definition and categorizing, but the definitions used by Wilson are appropriate to our purpose, and their application in primary education can be demonstrated.

The ability to treat others as equals and to have due consideration for them — or briefly, to love — has been shown by child development psychologists[2] to be a secondary experience that can only follow the initial experience of being loved. The good primary school, therefore, should appear to the child as a warm, accepting place where all individuals count, despite their differing abilities; where each child may have the opportunity to succeed, and where individual handicaps are absorbed by the community and compensated for. This suggests, too, that the teacher should have a pastoral role towards his class, with an oversight over each child's development. He should be accessible to them, possibly outside the school, in times of stress and when problems arise which affect his children.

Research into the effects of streaming would seem to indicate that an attitude of consideration towards others would be best experienced in a school organization which does not stream, label or categorize children.[3] Research has shown that there is always a tendency to live according to one's 'role expectancy'. Therefore, to label a child 'C' stream will often contribute to his remaining 'C' stream in ability and ambition. There may be situations in the classroom where competition would not be inherently inimical to the fostering of considerate and unselfish behaviour, but it may be dangerous for the teacher deliberately to prompt competition as an incentive in academic work, since this inevitably has the effect of discouraging those children who feel that by no amount of effort can they hope to shine as brightly as the clever ones. On the other hand, competition is an essential part of much physical education, and it may sometimes provide an incentive for effort in routine learning; but the teacher should try to ensure that where there is competition, it is not always the same children who fail. There are also occasions when competition may provide an outlet for aggression, and also the experience of losing and of failing in an area that is not too important for the child. It also appears that the right amount of stress may be valuable for the proper development of maturity. Failure is not always inherently undesirable. Some failure may contribute to the building of a realistic self-image, particularly for the child with average or above average ability. What is important is the child's attitude towards failure, and for children who feel rejected failure is a disincentive to learning. For such deprived children the teacher may need to provide opportunities of repeated success by carefully grading the work he sets. Thus, the child will gradually become persuaded of his ability to succeed. The richer and the more varied the school curriculum is, the more likely it is that every child will find something at which he can succeed. Thus, children may be given the opportunity to learn to respect and value others for what they *can* do, rather than to criticize, blame or denigrate others because of their failures. The teacher, then, may find it necessary to help some children to face failure without becoming unduly discouraged.

The ability to understand the feelings of oneself and of others can be fostered in the classroom situation by opportunities for group work where children are members of a small team producing a joint project, rather than always working as individuals thinking only of their own achievements or even as competitors against one another. Morality is concerned with interdependence, the relation of one's own interests with those of others and with the joint interest. This may be experienced in the discussion by the teacher and the class about the work to be undertaken, the allocation of tasks, the need to incorporate the lonely or the new child into group activity, and, for instance, the consideration of the interests of the cleaner or schoolkeeper when the children are engaged in messy, untidy work. Sympathetic understanding of other people can also be encouraged by appropriate story-telling, acting or miming that will provide vicarious experience where first-hand opportunities of meeting people are not available. At the infant or lower junior level, it is often possible to invite the actual 'people who help us' (school nurse, fireman, etc.) to talk to a class about their own work, but the upper juniors' sympathies should be extending beyond their immediate neighbours. This will frequently make direct experience impossible, and literature, biography and history will assume greater importance.

In the light of his experience in understanding the feelings of others, the child should also learn to think of the probable effects on others of any decision he has to make. He should learn to contribute his own experience and rational thinking to the formulation of agreed social rules. He should be encouraged to think about his own interests and ideals. These are all moral skills which can be fostered in later childhood by opportunities for discussion on the basis of the child's experience and by illustrations from real life or literature, radio, television or film. He becomes increasingly able to consider various opinions, and he is interested in adults' explanations of how they have reached a moral decision. From his understanding of the explanation, the child begins to generalize, utilizing his own experience and re-examining his own opinions. This suggests that the teacher should select material appropriate for the child's discussion and consideration, and which presents ideals worthy of his emulation which may be reinforced by reflection.

The ability to put into practice consideration of others, observance of the formulated social rules, and pursuit of one's personal ideals, is obviously the nub of moral education. It is one thing for a child to be convinced mentally of what he ought to do, quite another for him to do it. Even where a moral decision may be clear, self-interest may conflict with it overwhelmingly. There is often no clear moral imperative, and sooner or later the child has to learn that some moral problems have no absolute answer. Moreover, it is by no means clear whether the skill of putting moral rules into practice can be fostered by the school — apart from inducing conformity by punishment or adult pressures. If it can be done, how should it be done, and to what extent, since it is really an integral part of the individual personality structure? A classroom situation which provides the child with a share in deciding what work should be done, how the work should be tackled, and the encouragement to stick to a decided course of action for a reasonable length of time, seems more likely to help the growth of moral maturity than a very formal organization of work in which decisions are made by the timetable and the textbook. This would suggest that a carefully supervised day in which the teacher can cater for individual needs and guide children to make appropriate decisions and efforts, would provide useful experience of decision-making and of accepting responsibility for the consequences of decisions and that this might contribute to the development of moral practice. For instance, the teacher may initiate a study of local trees, but while following this theme one child may become sidetracked into an interest in the manufacture of paper from wood pulp. Rather than diverting him back to the main theme, the teacher would help him to explore this new interest and encourage the child to work on it, perhaps with the cooperation of a small group of his friends.

Experience shows, however, that any attempt at a daily programme in which the child is free to make his own decisions will only be successful in benefiting the child educationally if it is properly guided. A classroom environment in which maths equipment, reference books, art materials, and English corners are attractively presented will inspire most children to explore these with some enthusiasm. But the teacher must also be prepared to inspire interest where none existed before, to demonstrate the potentialities of the equipment provided, and to encourage the development of skills. Parallel with these educational objectives, such a classroom environment will give the children greater opportunities for social interaction amongst themselves than they would have in a formal classroom.

This, however, has its dangers as well as its benefits. With very young children and with those from insecure home backgrounds or no previous experience of freedom in the classroom, this method of organization can present serious difficulties until the children have developed to a certain degree the ability to treat each other with consideration. Unless their moral education at home has been very good, most primary children will inevitably put their own self-interest before that of others. Thus, a change from formal organization to integration must take place only gradually and under the control of an understanding teacher. Previous experiences may make it difficult for some children to adapt themselves to an atmosphere of comparative freedom.

Similar problems accompany cooperative or team teaching methods in which children may be free to visit the resource areas and teachers dealing with the subject of their choice. Many children need a great deal of direction, guidance and security, and thus they may also need one teacher in particular to whom they can turn, especially in times of stress. Many children tend to produce little or no work at all unless under constant stimulation and supervision, and provision must therefore be made to give such children special encouragement to achieve results and succeed in some field. In the cooperative teaching or in the integrated environment, such children may be overlooked, since they often have the appearance of being busy when they are not, in fact, learning or discovering anything.

In warning against its dangers we are not criticizing the method of cooperative teaching, which in addition to its encouragement of independence gives the child a more advanced social experience and social training than he can get in the traditional classroom. Also in this environment the child is not in danger of being condemned to a year with the wrong teacher, and the teacher is not condemned to suffer a year with a difficult class. There are disadvantages to some children, and we would deprecate any suggestion that all the educational answers are to be found in this method. Some examples of the method, with the arguments for and against, are well set out by one of our members.[4]

The good primary school, if it is to develop the moral qualities outlined here, must depend very heavily on the quality and enthusiasm of its teachers under the leadership of a head who is confident of the value of such methods. School buildings must also be adapted to the particular organization chosen, so that an open plan or suitable resource areas are possible under adult supervision. Within the controlled environment of such a school, many children may achieve the maturity to show consideration for other members of the school community and imagination in exercising initiative on behalf of others. By the end of the junior school they should be capable of discussing quite responsibly what are good or bad courses of action, and they are beginning to draw general principles of behaviour from specific examples and to put these into practice.

Notes
1. WILSON, J., WILLIAMS, N., and SUGARMAN, B. (1967) *Introduction to Moral Education*. Harmondsworth: Pelican.
2. For example: BOWLBY, J. (1953). *Child Care and the Growth of Love*. Harmondsworth: Penguin.
3. See: KAY, W. (1975). *Moral Education*. London: Allen & Unwin, pp. 268–70 and authorities cited p. 280.
4. PAPE, G.V. (1971). 'Cooperative Teaching in the Junior Department'. Occasional Papers on Primary Education, 19, March. Inner London Education Authority.

Part Two

The Curriculum

Chapter Four

Contributions of the Subject Areas

The established curriculum for young children already contains elements which can contribute to their moral education, that is, to produce the morally educated person as judged by the six criteria formulated by the Farmington Trust Research Unit, and mentioned at the beginning of the last chapter.[1] They may be rephrased as follows:

  a. He sees others as persons, whose interests are to be considered.
  b. He understands the way others feel about things (empathy).
  c. He can recognize the probable consequences of his own actions (foresight).
  d. He can generalize his experience to formulate rules of behaviour.
  e. He can see how a rule applies in a given situation to himself.
  f. He has enough control over his impulses to observe the rule in his own case.

To these Durkheim would have us add:

  g. He has a sense of duty and responsibility to the society and to the world in which he lives.[2]

In the early stages of education it is difficult to distinguish the 'matter' of what is taught from the 'manner' in which it is presented. Learning takes place through controlled exploration of a structured environment, rather than through 'subjects'. Traditional subject names such as 'history' or 'mathematics' may not appear on timetables, and the work of the children is developed from 'interests', 'topics', or 'projects' in which they become involved. Only in the later junior years may the disciplines of knowledge begin to be differentiated, although, as Comenius pointed out long ago, the elements of these disciplines are presented to the children from their earliest years.

The subject matter in the usual primary school curriculum might be roughly classified as follows:

1. Language Arts: oracy and literacy, speech and the skills of reading and writing; traditional and contemporary stories and poems; songs; at the junior stage, perhaps a foreign language.
2. Mathematics and Science: the discipline and uses of measurement; systematic description; the natural order; uses and abuses of knowledge.
3. Social Studies: different ways of living; conditions of development; social interdependence; other peoples; the neighbourhood; home economics.
4. Expressive Arts: creative activities of all kinds, imaginative play, drama, dance and movement, music, drawing, painting, modelling, crafts.
5. Assembly: meeting together of the school community to 'celebrate' its identity, to share in bringing together the life and work of the school.
6. Health Education: needs of the body; diet, use and abuse of drugs; physiology of sex, and its human meaning.
7. Religious Education: understanding one's own beliefs and beliefs by which others govern their lives.

What follows is a comment on each of these subject areas from the point of view of moral education, indicating how it may help to develop the moral characteristics a–g stated at the beginning of this chapter. In the context of this Report, RE has a separate chapter.

Language arts

In assisting the child to develop skills in oral communication and literacy the school builds on spontaneous talk by which children together create their shared social world. In due course writing enables them to withdraw, to record, to sort themselves out, to reflect on and evaluate their experiences.[3] The attention to what is said and written can be used to foster self-awareness and self-respect and awareness of and respect for others. Through language a world of persons is experienced and explored. With growing facility in reading and writing in the junior school years the child's opportunity to discover and examine the ideas of others increases. Where a second language is introduced the child's understanding is widened to include a culture different from his own (a,b).

The repertory of stories, rhymes, and songs which children enjoy are not important for any 'moral' they may have, but rather for their imaginative enlargement of the child's experience, which does have the moral effect of helping him to see what others see. However, even some simple stories present a moral problem of what to do, and he sees how the hero with whom he identifies himself resolves the question. He can be encouraged to reflect on this in the light of the consequences, and asked what he would have done, and why. To follow the repetitive pattern of some traditional stories is to rehearse the train of cause and consequence, e.g. 'The Old Woman and her Pig' (c).

Traditional stories and the nursery rhymes and folk songs which the children learn have an additional significance. They are part of the culture in which the child is growing up. He is being incorporated into a group which shares certain knowledge, traditions, customs, and literature. His self-identity is helped by seeing himself as belonging to an identifiable group (g). For this reason, it is thoughtless simply to assume that the school is an English school for English children, and that all the children share in this identity. Some of them may not. Sensitive recognition of children (any child) whose background is a different culture by bringing in some of their songs, verses, stories is not merely good manners, for it is necessary if they are to be helped to find a place and a part as members of the school community. A child can too easily be alienated and made to feel rejected by thoughtless disregard of his cultural identity, and the moral damage may be irreparable.

As reading skill develops, more avenues of understanding are opened. Infant and junior schools today have an abundance of books. The greater the variety, the wider the range of topics with which they deal, the more likely there will be something for everyone, as well as many windows on the world for the naturally curious. However, too many books at a time are too distracting or too daunting. A few selected for their attention at any one time give both books and children a better chance. History and geography introduced first as tales of 'far away and long ago' gradually become interesting as the human story (with geography as 'the other eye of history'). The child learns to work within the discipline imposed by the subject itself, to discern patterns of order and to accept methods of study.

So fundamentally important is reading, both as a social skill and as a gateway to exploration, that 'remedial reading' is the best moral education when it is needed. A child must not be allowed to fall chronically behind in this skill.

Mathematics and science

Through classifying, quantifying, ordering, the child is helped to see the structural relations of one thing to another, and glimpse the world as an ordered place. The persistence and accuracy required by all studies are measurable in mathematics: the answer is right or wrong; the problem is solved or not.

Plant life and animal behaviour are of immediate interest and accessibility and provide an inexhaustible field for accurate observation and description. The roots of ecology and ethology are found here: the cycle and balance of nature in the relations of organism and environment; the behaviour of animals is related to habitat, established for survival; the repertoire of each species is learned and transmitted, but there are exceptional individuals, a pattern that is seen again at a higher level in simple human communities.

Scientific knowledge is patiently won partly out of curiosity, to see the way things are, partly for 'the relief of man's estate'. Applied science, technology, has spectacular achievements, not merely in getting to the moon, but mainly in reducing the death rate and multiplying food production. These achievements have troublesome (perhaps catastrophic) side effects or other consequences: population pressures, the poisonous train of pesticides and herbicides, and all the other forms of pollution which damage the environment or upset natural balances.

Environmental studies are bound up with this first acquaintance with science as description of the natural world, and of the use that has been made of man's knowledge of it. This can be an introduction to the global tasks and problems which have brought mankind together, with recognized shared responsibility for the lives of generations of children unborn (g).

Social studies

Comparable with the different species of plants and animals in all their variety are the different human cultures which have existed and do exist. These amount to different ways of being human, for they are all cultures which have been developed by human beings in different geographical situations and with different equipments of knowledge and tools. The basis is economic: a way of life founded on a way of livelihood. Development depends originally on innovations and on a surplus; then on intercultural contacts in trading and by conquest.

Human interdependence is evident in any society, and is particularly complicated in modern industrial societies, after the division of labour, and after the insistence of workers (unions) on their independence. The claims of personal and group independence and the requirements of social interdependence have to be reconciled in acknowledged rights, enforceable as laws. Because of rapid and easy world-wide communications, a common technology, and the pressures of global problems, interdependence is now international.

Children very early should become acquainted with and come to terms with other children like themselves who have very different ways of living. Perhaps to very young children everyone else is strange, and even older children find plenty of differences to remark on in their acquaintances and neighbours. If other cultural groups are near at hand and send their children to the school, the differences are more striking and more general, and can be discussed and explained. Exchange visits to other countries, staying in the homes of foreign children and receiving them in return in their own homes, now often include junior children; they are of proved benefit in enlarging the experience of the children and stimulating their development.

Another option is to make a study of another people who are obviously different in race and culture, learning about the games, songs, clothes, food, homes, schools, family ways, holidays, of the other children, using visual aids and actual objects, and possibly corresponding with schools in this other part of the world. Partly, the young child is a natural anthropologist fascinated by other ways of behaving; partly, he is self-preoccupied, and remote differences do not interest him. So that this kind of project should not be imposed on children, and would be inappropriate at too early an age. When television and films have already begun to widen his horizon may be the time to begin to make contact with another culture.

'International exchanges of materials prepared by the pupils themselves, describing their environment and daily life, are an effective way of involving children directly in learning about their own and other countries and at the same time showing them that their knowledge, judgments and talents are respected.[4]

Junior children can try out cooking the dishes or doing the folk-arts of another culture, or can write their own impressions of life in the other children's world and send them for correction. The purpose is to gain understanding of other cultures and respect for them; superficial ideas and any belittlement are worse than ignorance.

Detailed study of a foreign community can be rich and rewarding, but should be planned thoroughly, not lightly undertaken. The cooperation of parents should be engaged. Teachers who are interested to do this would be well advised to consult *International Understanding in Primary Schools*, published by UNESCO in 1967 for the International Federation of Teachers' Associations.[5] This describes schemes, makes suggestions, and lists difficulties, based on experience gained by IFTA in various experiments in the Sixties. The booklet also contains two simplified versions of the United Nations Declaration of Human Rights by junior pupils in the USA and the UK, which provides a useful text for the discussion and understanding of independence and inter-dependence in the modern world.

To return home, the link of the school with the culture of the local community is important for the child's self-identity, as mentioned in Part One (p. 24). There should be ways of representing the neighbourhood in the curriculum, by local studies or projects, by bringing in West Indian arts and literature where there is a sizeable immigrant community, or otherwise.

Home economics represent in little the larger lessons of the experience of mankind. Any economy is a model: the balance of input and output, the reserves set aside out of surplus for contingencies or for expansion, the accountability; husbandry in expenditure and the use of resources. This simple model in the home can be directly related to the world scene, the flagrant waste of irreplaceable resources by the affluent nations, the deteriorating situation of the developing peoples; the widening gap, and the reckoning that is bound to come if the imbalance is not redressed. The simple economics of good management is a model of management, in a household, in national affairs, or in the conduct of life (a,c,d,g). All these topics are within the grasp of the older primary child, and valuable project work and discussion can result from them.

Expressive arts

It has been suggested that the modern world in valuing so highly its scientific and technological achievements has tended to underestimate the worth of the affective side of human personality. In the infant school the young child is stimulated to experiment with a whole range of expressive arts. Painting, drawing, modelling, constructing, drama (even the simplest imaginative play), dance and movement are everyday activities available to him. As with the language arts, the child is helped to express his ideas and feelings, using a variety of symbolic forms, which may come to him more easily than language. To the socializing value of this is to be added another use: the highly volatile emotions of the young child are canalized in an art form; he is able to express his feelings in a 'safe' manner, and control them. The Rosens remark on movement work: 'it seemed to have a remarkable effect on children's self-discipline and self-awareness and, in an indirect way, can affect much, even all, of the ways the children use language'.[6] The improvement of concentration and coordination by these methods may prove more successful than a direct attack on learning failures. Creative work demands planning and problem-solving to obtain the desired result, and persistence in effort. In drama or music or mural decoration this takes place in cooperation with others, which can give scope for spontaneity and originality disciplined by interdependence. In general, the expressive arts provide both intensely personal and shared group experiences (b,c,e,f).

Assembly

All the arts are available to celebrate all the themes of human existence at assemblies of the whole school. Until recently this was an untilled field because traditional morning assembly had been restricted to an act of Christian worship, and development was often inhibited by a too literal application of this statutory requirement. However, whatever the policy of the school in this matter, assembly can be a powerful influence on memorable occasions if it is treated imaginatively and not allowed to become a dull stereotyped performance.

The whole school present together has a corporate identity, and the child feels himself incorporated as a member of that body, with others older and younger than himself and with adults. Group experiences are powerful and formative, and this is the total group in his school life. If its performances are trivial, if his own participation in them is virtually excluded, the community itself can hardly be felt as worthwhile. On the other hand, if what is shared on these occasions is often evocative or impressive, and if he and his fellows are encouraged and helped to contribute their own ideas and feelings and concerns, he is likely to feel that this is a good community with which he wants to identify himself.

Although all the themes of human existence can furnish the topics of assembly, and some are regularly represented, such as the seasons, anniversaries, achievements, occasions, the life and work of the school and of the local community, the underlying structure is constant, and can be described by the words 'gathering', 'sharing', 'reflection'.

The sharing brings about discussion and dialogue, in assembly and afterwards in the classroom. What is to be shared has to be possessed, not imposed. Relationships of mutual trust and response are required to make this possible. Not only discussion, but also silence. School means subjection to a barrage of stimulus for a young child, and space and time are needed for detachment, reflection, assimilation. In assembly a short period of silence can be used, introduced by a sentence or two after the topic has been presented or discussed to focus reflection.

Some assemblies will stimulate an interest which may be followed up by individuals or groups, e.g., care of the environment arising out of a discussion about the school environment itself. In some schools all classes share responsibility on a rota basis for one or two assemblies each week. They may share with the whole school a topic which they have developed, and other classes may take it further. The language arts and the expressive arts have a manifest part in assembly programmes, but all the curriculum is involved. And older children represent themselves to younger ones, and the young ones to the seniors.

Many schools have varied the times when assembly is held. Although it is usual to open the day with assembly, some have found that this is not necessarily the best time every day of the week. Infant schools have found that the time immediately before the mid-morning break is good because the children have had an hour or so in school with their own class group actively engaged in their immediate interests before coming together for assembly. However, other times may be equally suitable, and each school will find its own way in its own circumstances.

There should be similar flexibility in the size of assembly. A child gains most from sharing with others in a group which is large enough to create a corporate experience, yet not so large as to frighten or bewilder. A nine-year-old may feel at home in a gathering which shocks a five-year-old by its sheer size; and the total community in a village school may be less than one-tenth the size of that in a large urban primary school. Appreciating the corporate experience, like most other aspects of personal growth, is a gradual and developing process; and in the large school especially there is reason for assemblies of differing composition, nature, and size.[7]

Health education

Care of the body is a basis of and focus for self-respect. This involves an adequate idea of what the body needs for health in diet, exercise, rest and change, cleanliness, routine checks. Most of this is taken care of in the health education programmes of primary schools. The underlying principles are well dealt with in the DES publications *A Handbook of Health Education* and *Movement: Physical Education in the Primary Years.*[8]

Drugs

A word is put in here about the use and abuse of drugs because for good and ill drugs are an increasingly available resource and recourse in our culture, and what should and should not be said about this in the education of our children is an important matter of concern.

Although children of twelve may begin taking pills recklessly, drugs are not usually thought of as a problem to be dealt with in the primary school. However, the recourse to drugs, more or less harmful, for relief or help is so easy and widespread that children do need to be given some early understanding of what is involved. In particular, smoking will begin with some children of primary school age. There are two ways in which primary education can and should help in the prevention of a drug problem: by identifying the vulnerable, and giving them special help; by beginning education in the use of drugs.

A school community engaged in enjoyed activities in which every child has a part and is stimulated and developed is the best that early education can provide in prevention of later addictions. In other words, education is itself a major contribution to the social control of drug abuse. But some children are specially vulnerable because they have had a bad start in life or are handicapped in some way in taking their proper part in the cooperation and competition of school life; they show signs of dropping out, of withdrawing into themselves. Such children do not necessarily come from deprived or obviously inadequate families. Teachers will want to do their best for these children because they are in need of special help. The additional risk in our society of drug dependence reinforces this natural wish to compensate the handicapped.

All children will know that aspirin and sleeping tablets and the like are used more or less frequently in the home; and they will know that tobacco and alcoholic drinks are in daily use throughout our society. They should learn that all such substances may be beneficial and may be harmful, that they are to be used only with care and discrimination. A doctor prescribes a drug with a specified dosage for a certain person in a given condition, and this is the model for a discriminating use of a medicinal drug, so that any other use may be described as abuse. In regard to the non-medicinal use of drugs, moderation is the rule. Perhaps the driver under the influence, driving without due care and attention, may be taken as a flagrant example of abuse. And people are known to damage their health and shorten their lives by excessive cigarette smoking or drinking. All these matters can be dealt with appropriately in the course of health education, and can be discussed openly and fully as need be. In our drug-dependent culture, this is as important an aspect of respect for the body as care of the teeth or personal hygiene or any other essential topic of health education. (For fuller treatment of the question, we would refer to the report of the Social Morality Council's working party, *Education and Drug Dependence.*[9])

Sex education

Education in bodily functions can also be a starting point for education in the wider subject of sex, with what that implies for personal relationships as children grow. We agreed that something should be done in a straightforward way to inform children in the junior school about human reproduction. This should be done in the context of some general course, and the topic should not be singled out for treatment in isolation. We also agreed that when the physiological facts were dealt with explicitly, as they should be, the manner should not be clinical but should convey the warmth of intimate human relationships and family life.

We saw with some enthusiasm an audio-vision programme produced by the BBC for young children.[10] The headmistress who had devised the programme and who demonstrated it to us had shown it first to her own staff and then to the parents of all the children to whom it was proposed to show it. Not only did the parents approve of the programme, they found it a talking-point which encouraged them to bring out and discuss family matters that concerned them. The occasion opened a new relationship between school and home. The material itself demonstrated the practicability of a warm human approach to these facts of life; and although the teaching programme was not in a family context, involvement of the family in the programme made it likely that it would be discussed at home.

In the course of our discussions on sex education, we invited Dr Jack Dominian[11] to communicate his views, and with grateful acknowledgement we reproduce the later part of a paper which he submitted.

'Traditionally, when the body is mentioned in the context of sexual education it is invariably assumed that the reference is to the physical differences between the sexes, the mechanism of sexual arousal, intercourse, fertilization, pregnancy and birth. Before discussing any of these it is worth remembering that the characteristics . . . figuring at the centre of love, namely, the ability to trust, give and receive recognition and appreciation, reassurance, comfort, encouragement, and forgiveness, which are part of the process of sustaining, healing and growth in personal relationships, are largely mediated through the body. Physical touch conveys all these, and the ability to educate the growing person to accept his body and that of others as a means of communicating feelings of care and love, rather than warning them from their earliest years of the dangers of impurity, is one of the real challenges of sexual education at home and school.

'The acceptance of the body in a positive and appreciative manner depends on the ability of parents and teachers to answer truthfully, frankly and accurately the child's questions which may begin as early as the third year and will continue thereafter uninterruptedly, centred on two main themes, namely: Where do I come from? How did I get there? And a subsidiary one which is of greater importance for girls: How did I get out?

'These questions will appear in a fragmented sort of way, arising out of chance incidents such as the birth of domestic animals, stories, and, far more important, events such as the arrival of a younger brother or sister or the pregnancy of a member of the staff. Children ask the same questions repeatedly, and the key to sexual education is to repeat the answers with the same consistency of truthfulness, in increasing elaboration.

'Sometime about the age of nine onwards the child is capable of comprehending a coherent sequence of the sexual encounter. The anatomical differences between the sexes, leading to physical closeness, penetration of the female by the male, sexual intercourse, the emission of semen, the fertilization of ovum and sperm, the gestation, the growth of the foetus in the uterus, the enlargement of the uterus, the special construction of the female pelvis to accommodate the foetus, its progress into the outside world in labour, the role of doctors, midwives, hospital, home confinement and the care of the baby, form an essential chronicle of the main anatomical and psychological events.

'The facts are pieces of information relating to whole people and should be frequently related to significant people in the life of the child, so that the wonder and fascination of the body are coupled with the wonder and fascination of personal encounter.

'This ideal of harmony between physical knowledge and personal significance requires a close liaison between school and parents. So much of sexual education depends on the attitude and value conveyed about physical facts that there must be a close understanding between home and school.

'This understanding will ensure some uniformity in the level of information conveyed. The child should not be exposed to the violent contradiction of utter silence in one and a flood of information in the other. He may draw all sorts of conclusions about the discrepancy. Information from the two sources should be roughly the same and the language reasonably similar, which is best achieved by sticking to correct terminology. Such vocabulary needs to include at least such words as sperm, ovum, penis, scrotum, vagina, uterus, umbilical cord, foetus, pregnancy, sexual intercourse, breasts, nipples, lactation . . .

'The school staff consists of men and women who act as teachers, catering staff, those who assist at meals, caretakers, sometimes a nurse. All these people form part of the living community within which the child grows. This community is of course a sexual community in the sense that the members express the whole range of the single, married, parents, widows, widower . . . The single may get engaged and married. Some teachers may become pregnant and have a baby. Others in the older group may lose their spouses. A few may experience a serious illness of their spouse or children . . . Any school that is truly committed to the task of sexual education must look at itself as a sexual community in which the lives and experiences of the staff impinge on the life of the children as the life of the parents does on the children of the individual family. This reality is a difficult one to recognize or face, but any commitment towards openness and integrity of sexual education which seriously bypasses the sexual values, attitudes, and experiences of the education is as much a deception as the conspiracy of silence in the past . . .'

Sexual morals are perhaps no longer thought of as what morality is about, and are not the main content of morality, and relations between the sexes are not usually urgent in primary schools, but they will become so, and when behaviour is under that strain the seven ethical criteria (a–g) are pre-eminently and peremptorily relevant.

This survey of the curriculum from the point of view of moral education is intended merely to show that each subject area may make a distinctive contribution to moral understanding, and in some cases to the formation of moral habits; and to illustrate ways in which this may be done. This is no more than pointing the way. The usefulness of the curriculum for moral education depends upon the teacher's awareness of that use and readiness to bear in mind the specific objectives of moral education as suggested at the beginning of this chapter. These are not seven commandments on tables of stone, but they make sense, are not vulnerable to serious challenge, are not likely to violate anybody's conscience, and indeed are requisites of the kind of society we are used to and value. Unless some clear objectives are formulated and worked to, any good moral result of our educational work is happy accident – if indeed without criteria we could recognize a good result.

Notes
1. WILSON, J., WILLIAMS, N. and SUGARMAN, B. (1967). *Introduction to Moral Education*. 192–5. Harmondsworth: Penguin. See also: Harold Loukes' paper 'What is moral education?'. In: MACY, C. (Ed) *Let's Teach Them Right.* London: Pemberton.
2. DURKHEIM, E. (1961). *Moral Education.* New York: Glencoe Free Press.
3. ROSEN, C. and H. (1973) *The Language of Primary School Children*, pp. 43, 142, and 149. London: Penguin Education for the Schools Council.
4. *Education for International Understanding and Peace, with Special Reference to Moral and Civic Education*. Report of a Meeting of Experts. (1970). Paris: UNESCO ED/MD/17.
5. INTERNATIONAL FEDERATION OF TEACHERS' ASSOCIATIONS. (1967). *International Understanding in Primary Schools*. Paris: UNESCO.
6. *Ibid.*, p. 196.
7. Help with the new approach to Assembly can be found in:
   WETZ, P. (1974). *Celebrating Together.* London: Longman. A resource book for primary assemblies.
   HULL, J. (1975). *School Worship: an Obituary.* London: SCM Press.
   Wider Horizons. (1972) London: British Humanist Association. Suggestions for modern assemblies.
8. DEPARTMENT OF EDUCATION AND SCIENCE. (1968). *A Handbook of Health Education.* London: HMSO.

DEPARTMENT OF EDUCATION AND SCIENCE. (1976). *Physical Education in the Primary Years*. London: HMSO.
9. SOCIAL MORALITY COUNCIL WORKING PARTY. (1975). *Education and Drug Dependence*. London: Methuen.
10. *School Broadcasting and Sex Education in the Primary School*. (1971). London: BBC for the School Broadcasting Council.
    SHEFFIELD, M. (1973). *Where Do Babies Come From?* London: Cape. Adapted from BBC Radiovision Series.
11. DOMINIAN, J. M.B., B.Chir, MRCPE, DPM, MRC Psych. Consultant Psychiatrist, Central Middlesex Hospital; Director of Marriage Research Centre, Central Middlesex Hospital; Medical Adviser to Catholic Marriage Advisory Council; author of *Marital Breakdown*. (1968). Harmondsworth: Penguin; and *The Church and the Sexual Revolution*. London: Darton, Longman & Todd.

Chapter Five

Religious Education

A modern approach

Any discussion on religious education must start with acceptance by those taking part of the reality of the present position in this country. It can no longer be assumed that this is a 'Christian' country, in the sense that there is no need to take account of or pay regard to other beliefs and ways of life. From a very early age children, even from the most sheltered homes, are made aware of the existence of other ways of thinking and behaving than those taught by their parents. The fact that children are influenced by the mass media from early years is another potent factor in making them aware of the pluralist society in which they live. The educational procedures which have been developed in recent years have all aimed at challenging children to independence of thought and action, to freedom of discussion. Even if we wished to do so, it would be impossible to present religious education by any other than an 'open' approach.

Intolerance and dislike for people unlike ourselves is generally the result of ignorance and fear. An early initiation into an awarenesss of the variety of mankind's cultures and religions would surely go a long way towards counteracting ignorance, opening young minds to an acceptance of ways of life outside their immediate experience, and towards engendering a liking for all men in their infinite diversity. A group of white London secondary school girls attended a school where there were West Indians but no Asians. The West Indians were accepted but the girls were sure that 'Pakis' were dirty, never washed, were infested with lice, and always eat 'smelly' food. Of what use is literacy, numeracy, religion, and the whole range of school subjects if they leave young people so grossly ignorant of their fellow men? We all now have to share the same world, learn to live as one human race, to accept our differences and agree to live with them.

But it is at this point, for those holding traditional views, that the precise difficulty arises. Religious belief does not, in the view of believers, derive solely from experience; whilst it cannot be alien to, divorced from, nor irrelevant to experience, it always contains an element of the 'given', that which is 'revealed'. This is as true of Christianity as of other faiths. It is important to remember, however, as the 'Note of Reservation on Religious Education' in the Plowden Report points out[1] that theology is a recondite subject which only the adult mind is capable of studying (which is a comment on technique and language rather than on content; a teacher of RE can no more avoid theological implications than a teacher of ethics can avoid reference to human behaviour). By its very nature formal theology can have no place in the education of young children. It is necessary therefore to examine the bases from which theological formularies have been developed.

All religions are concerned with a whole way of life and are therefore rooted in fundamental human experience. The experiences of birth, of growing up, of love, of companionship, of success and failure are common to all, and are the formative experiences of the young. At the major points of his existence man is brought face to face with deep questions about his own significance and destiny. The very fact that he fails so often to achieve, despite all his efforts, the ideals of justice, equity, peace and brotherhood, raises questions which have to be faced. It is reflection on these experiences and these questions that is the background to the development of religious thought.

Yet these are adult reflections and can have little significance for children. The child is involved in their results of course in a manner appropriate to his stage of development. This is particularly true with regard to his participation in the festivals and ceremonials which belong to his culture. If the religious festivals and ceremonials are examined carefully it will be seen that each in some way celebrates one of these fundamental 'life experiences'. For example, the Christian celebration of Easter is more than a memorial of an event, it is the Christian's affirmation of his belief in the presence of the risen Christ in his life, and is a reflective celebration of his own experience of death and resurrection, of success growing out of failure. For the Jew the celebration of the Passover feast is an opportunity, through reliving in ritual form a deeply significant event of their history, to reflect on his people's trust in divine providence and the covenant which ruled their destiny. In keeping Ramadhan the Muslim learns the value of self-discipline and commemorates the sending down of the Qur'an as the guide to life. In sharing with the adults of the community in these festivals, however denuded or commercialized some of them may have become, the child is brought into touch with the deeps of human life as experienced and interpreted by his own people.

It is not only in the high moments of life, however, that the child can be helped to develop what might be called a 'religious' attitude to life. No one can give a child 'faith', but what parents and teachers can do is to help the child to think deeply about his own life experiences, so that questioning and searching may grow and not be stifled by premature answering of questions he is not even aware enough to ask.

Those who fear this open approach to religious education in the school should remember that the young child is growing up within the community of the home, and in some cases of the church or religious group. Therefore he will inevitably interpret his school and other experiences in relation to these communities to which he belongs. His attitudes will be influenced from the beginning by those with whom he is closely associated. The child's very uniqueness develops through association with his communities. Their ways of life will be passed on to him long before he can understand the bases on which these rest. As he grows older he will need to understand these beliefs or principles so that he can evaluate and then accept or reject them for himself.

Christianity in primary education

For children in this country some knowledge of Christianity would seem to be an essential part of their religious education, for our culture rests at least partially on Judeo-Christian foundations. At what stage of development and in what way the children are best introduced to these facts is for each teacher to decide.

Story telling has a traditional place in religious education. Stories have always been a vehicle in which norms and values have been handed on. Of even greater importance, perhaps, is the fact that many traditional stories deal in a symbolic manner with the fundamental experiences of life mentioned earlier. 'Stories hold religious significance because they mirror nature and human needs.'

For many years it was assumed that the presentation of bible stories was the best 'method' of religious education for children. In view of the unique place the Bible holds in the tradition of our country this would appear to be valid. Recent research, however, has shown that this approach can have special difficulties. Many of these may well be overcome by careful selection of material and good teaching. However, the question remains as to whether it is advisable to introduce young children to biblical material before they have some understanding of different literary forms. Young children generally interpret material literally, and misunderstandings formed in the early years may be difficult or even impossible to eradicate. This may well inhibit them from coming to any real understanding and appreciation of the Bible in adolescence and later life.

In more recent years, to avoid these dangers, a 'life theme' approach has been introduced.[2] This also has the advantage that it attempts some integration of 'subject areas'. Studies of schemes produced for this type of teaching tend, however, to give the impression that 'religion' is being 'dragged in' — or alternatively is entirely absent. It is as if there is an acknowledged dichotomy between 'religion' and 'life' which somehow must be bridged. Those who have a religious attitude to life do not acknowledge such a dichotomy. Religion and life cannot be separated if one is an interpretation of the other. Whether or not religious language is used, the values are what matter. 'The study of deserts, dust bowls, irrigation schemes, re-afforestation projects is concerned with man's stewardship of natural resources; learning about work among those who are starving or homeless because of flood or drought involves man's responsibility for his fellow man. These are religious values; they are not made religious, they are not even made more religious by reference to the bibilical concept of man's domination over nature or to the parables of the Good Samaritan and the Sheep and the Goats' (Jean Holm). They are religious values at least in the sense that these are the human values chosen and cherished by some of the world religions, by Christianity in particular.

The development of concepts and of an appreciation of values is only a part of religious education. The child needs help to develop as a sensitive and aware human being. His imaginative and emotional life is fostered in a good primary school through a variety of creative activities. The emphasis today on technological achievement makes the provision of these kinds of experience even more necessary than they were in the past. The ability to enjoy things just for what they are, and not for what men can do with them, needs to be developed early. These experiences, too, help to develop the sensitivity which religious thinking requires, for the religious and the aesthetic seem to be closely related.

Much emphasis has been laid on the necessity of providing suitable experiences for the children. What is not so often stressed is the equally necessary provision of opportunities for the children to reflect on their experiences. In the noisy world of the twentieth century silence is a novelty in itself for our children. We need to ensure that the children not only share a communal period of quiet and reflection but also have the chance to be 'quiet' on their own at times. With the increasing development of open-plan schools it is vital that 'quiet places' be provided where a child can withdraw physically to develop his own thoughts in peace.

In sum, Bible teaching, theme teaching, the cultivation of life-experiences provide different methods of religious education none of which is sufficient, each of which has dangers as well as usefulness.

All this imposes exacting demands on the teacher for understanding and skill. In the secondary school specialist teachers in RE are becoming more common. These teachers have had the opportunity to study more deeply the advances in child psychology as well as in biblical and theological knowledge, and the fundamentals of other world religions. They are therefore able to help the young adolescent in his questioning search for the truths on which he is to build his own life. The primary school teacher has no such advantage. Religious education is yet another rapidly developing area with which the 'all purpose' teacher is supposed to be able to cope. This is not a plea for specialist teachers in RE for the primary school, but rather a case for one member of the school staff to be given the opportunity to acquire special qualifications in this field in order to act as adviser and support for the others. The Christian Education Movement provides courses for primary teachers, resource material, and an advisory service, organized nationally and regionally.

The place of world religions in the curriculum
   Children at the infant and junior stages of development cannot be expected to grasp the intricacies of belief and symbolism involved in religious practices. Indeed, these are not always understood by the adults who practise them. Nevertheless, children can appreciate that the outward appearances of religion in various cultures are also varied, and as long as the teacher's attitude towards them is both sympathetic and serious, the children will also learn to respect even that which appears strange.
   Children can enter into the atmosphere of different places of worship, respond to music, art, stories and poetry. Not only will they receive these as information, but they may also, under the guidance of a skilled teacher, respond to the religious feelings which have so often inspired these arts. At the same time, children may learn about the dress, food, customs and homes of different peoples as well as their temples and ways of worship. They will not then look upon the Muslim's way of saying his prayers as being strange or funny, neither would they ridicule a Sikh's turban or a Roman Catholic's act of crossing himself.
   Clearly, specialists in such fields as geography, history, English literature, art and social studies have much to contribute to this work, as well as the specialist in religious education. In fact, a good primary teacher needs to have some knowledge of all these fields. The average primary teacher, however, cannot be expected to have such a wide range of knowledge, nor can he be interested in so many subjects. There is much to be said for the teacher to make his approach through the particular subject which interests him personally, since his enthusiasm

will generally inspire the children too.

The resources available to the teacher both for his own information and for use in the classroom are still somewhat scattered and thin on the ground. Nevertheless, these are increasing day by day and a teacher with a real interest in the subject will be able to create and collect much material for himself. It is important to remember that infant and junior children, and a great many secondary children too, are not interested in wordy accounts or in reading books for themselves, but they will respond best to simple stories, pictures, exhibitions of objects, colourful models, films and slides. A list of sources for such materials is given at the end of this chapter.

Dangers in the teaching of world religions

In our plural society there is danger in not teaching about world religions — the danger of prejudice. But when this teaching is undertaken there are certain risks to be borne in mind and guarded against.

1. The first is the presentation of stereotypes. This can easily happen when people underestimate the wealth and complexity of cultures other than their own. It is a dangerous form of misrepresentation and it leads people to adopt attitudes towards a large part of the religious experience of mankind formed by the mistaken impression that they have studied it and know all about it.

2. The second danger is conscious or unconscious misrepresentation. This may arise from the use by the teacher of unsatisfactory sources of information, and from sheer ignorance. It may also arise from his open or hidden desire to 'teach for a verdict' in favour of his own religious viewpoint. It may result from his understandable but unsuccessful attempt to make simple what is really complex, or it may misrepresent by being untypical, e.g. giving children the impression that all Hindus live in squalor, or that all Muslims are polygamous.

3. Closely related to this is misunderstanding by the pupils. It must be remembered constantly that the child will interpret what he sees and hears in the light of his own previous experience — the experience of a child, not an adult. A junior child is not ready to cope with adult concepts. He may seriously misunderstand the customs and beliefs of others, especially if these belong to an alien culture. This may not be a serious matter, so long as there are opportunities at a later stage for these misconceptions to be removed. What must be avoided is the kind of misunderstanding which leads to fixed attitudes and a closed mind.

4. One common tendency is to trivialize world religions, or to present just bits and pieces, leaving the impression that they are all rather curious and odd. This can easily happen if the emphasis is simply

on externals. Religious education must transcend the informative. Children need to gain insight into the human, experiential dimension of religion, to meet and come to appreciate people who are believers, and to encounter literature, poetry and art that conveys the quality and the feeling underlying what religious people say and do.

5. The use of people who are believers presents its own problems, whether they be visitors to the classroom or pupils within the class. The chief thing to remember is that they are not a substitute for the teacher. They are one form of 'resource material'. The teacher must decide what is the best use to make of them, and whether their contribution helps or hinders a balanced presentation of the religion in question.

6. Any tendency to syncretism should be avoided. It is a mistake to suppose that all religions are variants of something called Religion, with a capital 'R', or that all religions are really looking for the same things. The school's business is to promote real understanding of religions as they are. This cannot be achieved if their distinctive natures are obscured by some scheme to draw out the 'highest common factor'.

7. 'The new RE is concerned with initiating young people into the meaning of religion and religions, and not only the Christian religion . . . In brief, the new RE tries to stare facts in the face and to present the living world in all its rich plurality. Sympathy, criticism, plurality — these are some of the slogans the teacher needs to use in adapting his understanding to that of the pupils . . . Further, it is useless to discuss religion or to look deeply into it without recognizing that there is a strong agnostic and atheistic 'secular' strand in the modern world. It is absurd, for one cannot insulate pupils from the actual world . . .' (Professor Ninian Smart).

This non-religious view of the world, and the attitudes that go with it, are not merely modern. In the Graeco-Roman world, long before Christianity, Epicurus taught and practised a simple humanism; and he was the first to welcome women and slaves into his fellowship. Humanists have consistently stressed certain virtues and values: to tolerate different beliefs, to promote happiness in the world, to cultivate friendship, to inquire into the nature of everything, to develop and use the arts and sciences to fight against ignorance, poverty, and disease. Their contribution to civilization should not be overlooked in introducing children to the convictions by which men live.

8. Teachers sometimes tend to assume that because a subject has been introduced to a class, it has registered, and the children then know about it. The truth is that many things do not register at all the first time, and much of what is done needs to be repeated in as vivid a manner as possible before either its content or its meaning becomes clear to the children. This is as true of religion and culture as it is of

mathematics. Thus, the teacher must take care to introduce only a little
at a time and only that which is within the grasp of his pupils at their
particular stage of mental development. Too much introduced too
rapidly may easily confuse children and lead to subsequent
misunderstanding.

Promoting tolerance and understanding

At all ages, when world religions and non-religious convictions are
studied it is important to foster an attitude of tolerance and a
willingness to stand where the other person stands in an effort to see
how something must appear to him. There is a danger that without an
attempt to reach this empathetic standpoint, the study of different
convictions may produce only negative results. Tolerance and
understanding will be achieved most effectively by personal contact,
and in the absence of that, by a skilful use of literature and by the
teacher's encouragement of sensitive relationships within the classroom
and the school. The fostering of these positive attitudes in the children
will then extend, we hope, outside the school into the wider
community.

Notes
1. DEPARTMENT OF EDUCATION AND SCIENCE. CENTRAL ADVISORY
   COUNCIL FOR EDUCATION. (ENGLAND). (1967). *Children and their
   Primary Schools*. (Plowden Report). 1, 489—92. London: HMSO.
2. HOLM, J. (1966). 'Life themes — what are they?', *Learning for Living*, 9, 2,
   15—18.

Sources of Information for Materials
HILL, J. (Ed). (1971). *Books for Children: The Homelands of Immigrants in
Britain*. London: Institute of Race Relations. Bibliography.

LIBRARY ASSOCIATION. YOUTH LIBRARIES GROUP. (1971). *Books for the
Multiracial Classroom: a Select List of Children's Books Showing the Backgrounds
of India, Pakistan and West Indies*. London: Library Association.

SCOPE: *An Introductory English Course for Immigrant Children. Handbook 1:
The Social Background of Immigrant Children from India, Pakistan and Cyprus*.
(1970). London: Longman. This is a publication from the Schools Council project
on English for Immigrant Children, University of Leeds.

TRUDGIAN, R. (1973). *Community Relations*. Probe No. 14. The religious life
of immigrant comunities in Britain. London: SCM Press for the Christian
Education Movement.

WOODWARD, P. (Ed). (1973). *World Religions: Aids for Teachers*. London:
Community Relations Commission. Contains sections on audiovisual aids, useful
addresses, calendar of religious festivals, lists of books. Information is given about
the SHAP Working Party which produced the material and exists to help world
religions in education.

Chapter Six

Themes and Doctrines, Ancient and Modern

Any assumption that what belongs to the 'childhood of the race' ought to be suitable for young children is quite a mistake. Legend is not history for children. Nature and culture myths are not simple introductions to modern knowledge about the origins of man and his eventual discoveries and inventions. Myths and legends may offer good stories, but their 'meaning' is bound up with ways of feeling and thinking buried in the past, and often obscured by later revisions. Study of them is a difficult and tentative new subject. In history or in science it is possible and desirable from the beginning to lay foundations in simple factual outline which can be grasped by the young, and gradually filled in during the school course.

Teachers are not well advised, therefore, merely to follow the beaten paths in dealing with traditional material in all its variety: myths, legends, fables, folk-tales, proverbs, parables, allegories. A good story is a good story, whatever its provenance or its esoteric meaning, and can be chosen for its entertainment or imaginative value. In general, the point of a fable, folk-tale, or proverb is a piece of earthy wisdom that comes home readily to young children. In general, the allegory and the parable depend on contexts outside a young child's experience. The Good Samaritan is a good story, but the point is missed if it is taken as simply about helping somebody in distress, exemplified in a thousand other stories. There is no good reason why myths and legends should be told and retold simply because they have come down the ages; myths that were once believed or half-believed, like the Labours of Hercules, because they expressed needs or aspirations, and no longer do so, or have been allegorized, like the Garden of Eden. Products of imaginations far away and long ago are not likely to retain immediacy. On the other hand, fables and myths of our own time (e.g., *Animal Farm* or *Lord of the Flies*[1] or the legendary James Dean) are rather obviously suitable only for more advanced study and discussion.

The approach in school to traditional material in general has been challenged by the question of the Bible in particular, which abundantly exemplifies it all. The problem of handling the Bible intelligently and intelligibly with young children has seemed so formidable that enlightened practice has tended to leave it alone. Ronald Goldman, as an outcome of his investigations, warned primary teachers off by showing the inescapable danger of engendering ineradicable misunderstandings before the child is of an age to form concepts.[2] There was then a tendency to resort to a 'life theme' approach, as mentioned in the last chapter, deploying topics like 'light' or 'bread' or 'water' as images or themes which explore and link experiences that are universal and profound, and which illuminate or are illuminated by a religious interpretation. Whether or not this method of encouraging and training preconceptual thinking has proved its worth, it is not an answer to the main question about the use of the Bible in primary schools. Is it for school purposes a magazine of edifying stories, or has it the coherence of a theme which it should be the main purpose to bring out: is it a quarry or a building? Goldman himself calls for a clear frame of reference, especially in any introduction to biblical history in the Old Testament.

Quarrying material from the Bible for use in the classroom was natural when it could be reasonably assumed that the children had a good idea of what it was all about. If that familiarity cannot be assumed, a reasonable teacher will begin by trying to give them some idea of what it is about. But what is the frame of reference that makes contemporary sense? The picturesque simplicity of Milton's epic, the Fall of the Angels followed by Paradise Lost and Paradise Regained, is not merely mythical; the myth is too concrete and too remote to carry current credit. Any attempt to demythologize would be a rash excursion into theology. A fundamentalist view of the Bible as literal truth is equally inadmissible in the classroom. The Bible is of course a composite work, a literature not a book, and some understanding of how it is made up, with an appreciation of the time-scale and the dating of the documents, is required of any teacher who would use it for the purposes of religious education. But the books of the Bible are within two covers because they are bound together by certain beliefs and purposes.

The main theme of the OT can be taken as the covenant of the God of Israel with his chosen people, whose loyalty and obedience would be blessed with all good. This begins with the relations of a nomadic desert tribe with their war-god, the Lord of Hosts, a jealous tribal god who demands for his favours exclusive loyalty as well as the usual 'burned offerings, with calves of a year old'. They are delivered out of Egypt and given a land flowing with milk and honey, but when they are despoiled and deported by more powerful peoples and their hope is defeated that the Lord of Hosts will put their enemies under their feet, they learn why the Lord has turned his face from Israel: 'He hath showed thee, O man, what is good; and what doth the Lord require of thee but to do justly, and to love mercy, and to walk humbly with thy God?' (*Micbah*, 6, 8). The remnant returns to recover their inheritance and wait for forgiveness, their nationhood shattered. The biblical blend of history with myth and legend shows a people who are being taught by bitter experience to concentrate on fellow feeling and social justice and humble dependence on a God who required only these things and would not reward propitiatory gifts with worldly success. The heroes, from Abraham to Ezra, are those who remain faithful and hopeful whatever befalls. The theme is rich in stories and personalities and colourful language; and it is the interpretation of human experience which brought into the world the promise of the theological virtues of faith, hope, and charity to match, or to challenge, the tried cardinal virtues of wisdom, courage, temperance, and justice. Sanctification of humility in service, a transvaluation of worldly values, was the message of Christianity to the world which for example, inspired Chivalry (the model followed by St Francis), idealized the feudal social contract ('my station and its duties' in Langland's *Piers the Plowman*[3]), and, in a later social order, the stewardship of the 'Protestant ethic'.

However historical the theme, it may seem far removed from the experience and interest of primary school children, as remote as any of the esoteric myths, and therefore something that it would not be wise to trouble them with. After all, these are adult concepts and Goldman's warning holds. In particular, the theme is one of historical development, which children cannot conceptualize. However, they can see development in plants and animals. They can understand that men lived and behaved differently in former times as in other places. Otherwise, a great deal of what is done without question every day in primary schools would be worse than a waste of time. If the Bible is talking about life, if Jesus speaks of losing one's life to find it, that is because of this experience of a people which is pieced together in the OT, an experience proclaimed and interpreted in a way that made it of universal significance.

Neglect of this core theme makes it impossible to deal with the Bible at all as the source of a main tradition of European culture. We are not saying: teach this theme. We are saying: children in primary schools can grasp what the Bible is about if they are given a clue; that the clue is in the historical experience of a people, as they learned to understand it, narrated in the OT; that this had an outcome narrated in the NT which issued in the Christian message to the world which has founded churches and made revolutions, and inspired endeavour and achievement far beyond the place and time of these origins. Many children will not be able to make sense of what they do hear about the Bible or about Christianity unless they are introduced early to an outline of the background.

The other main theme, which is of more general application as a criterion of selection and as the core of all studies, is the story of the evolutionary development of man on the planet, against the background of the stellar universe. There is both the theory of the biological evolution of species and the history of cultural development.

Again, all this may seem a proper study for later on and entirely out of place in primary schools. Again, it is suggested that in outline the story is concrete and interesting, and that foundations should be laid at this stage of education because this is the frame of reference and the coordinating principle of all subsequent studies.

The immense time-scale could be conveyed in simple models, and not merely by unimaginable figures. There is now abundant graphic material for picturing what has happened in evolution and cultural development.[4]

Human civilization thus far has been only one tick of the cosmic clock, but even within civilization the world has been transformed in the short space of a generation. Mr. Wedgwood Benn, when he was Minister of Technology, liked to project this dramatic change of tempo by showing diagrams of what the invention of machines has done for travel, communication, killing, and calculating, from the zero of walking, speaking, hand-to-hand combat, and counting on the fingers, to supersonic flight, telecommunication (a news flash on every editor's desk around the world in four minutes), nuclear weapons, and computers. In each case the graph rises steeply to near vertical from near horizontal in the period since the war.[5] This sudden change of tempo does not diminish the importance of the wheel or the compass or gunpowder or the steam engine, nor does this explosion of knowledge abolish the classical evils of ignorance, poverty, and disease; but the perspective of human history is abruptly altered, and mankind is brought together in face of new formidable cultural tasks and problems of the greatest moral consequence. Have we updated our more elementary school texts to take due account of these far-reaching changes of our time?

The invention of machines is of course only one aspect of the growing power of man over his environment. On the biological map, each species adapts to, explores, and exploits its habitat, its living space; on the cultural map, each human community does likewise. With the contacts and intercourse of cultures comes the stimulus to development that produces inventions, and their diffusion that brings about the advancement of the race, till relatively helpless if ingenious adaptation to the environment becomes domination and exploitation which loses sight of the close and necessary dependence of human existence on the habitat. Mankind is learning painfully and dangerously to be responsible for human life.

This evolutionary and ecological thinking about man's long development, and the dramatic turn in his position and responsibility, can hardly begin too soon if it is introduced sensibly and in concrete terms that are interesting and impressive and simple to grasp. This perspective, this truth about man is a challenge to the teacher, not a syllabus. Of course the concepts of evolution and of historical development are beyond the child at the preconceptual stage, but that is no reason why they should not inform the primary curriculum in appropriate ways. Graphic, episodic treatment can help to lay foundations, but whatever detail is used at this stage should not be a charge on the memory, should be used simply to form an impression of the way things are, or convey a sense of how it came about; accurate learning comes later.

Above all, these major themes are clues for the teacher, frames of reference, criteria of relevance for the selection and rejection of material and the treatment of topics, not subjects for explicit, insistent, examinable teaching. What is wanted is imaginative preparation, a preliminary look at what the world is like, a preface to the introduction to great questions which school education ought to be.

Notes
1. ORWELL, G. (1965). *Animal Farm*. London: Longman.
   GOLDING, W. (1954). *Lord of the Flies*. London: Faber.
2. GOLDMAN, R. (1964). *Religious Thinking from Childhood to Adolescence*. London: Routlege & Kegan Paul.
3. LANGLAND, W. (1965). *Piers the Plowman*. London: Macmillan.
4. For example: Mitchell Beazley's, *The Atlas of the Earth* (1972). The part called 'The Good Earth' is a mine of diagrams and pictorial representations of the history and structure of the earth and its inhabitants.
5. 'Machines and people'. In: *Towards an Open Society: Ends and Means in British Politics*. (1971). London: Pemberton. Proceedings of a Seminar Organized by the British Humanist Association.

9826